1996

In Memory of

DEAN F. FENTON

MARY COTTON PUBLIC LIBRARY
SABETHA, KANSAS

★ SPORTS STARS ★

REGGIE MILLER

BASKETBALL SHARPSHOOTER

By Ted Cox

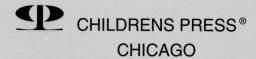

CHILDRENS PRESS®
CHICAGO

Photo Credits

Cover, ©Scott Cunningham/Sportschrome East/West; 5, ©Noren Trotman/ Sports Photo Masters, Inc.; 6, ©Scott Cunningham/Sportschrome East/West; 9, ©Noren Trotman/Sports Photo Masters, Inc.; 10, ©Rick Stewart/Allsport USA; 13, ©Jon SooHoo/USC Sports Information; 15 (top), AP/Wide World; 15 (bottom), 16, Courtesy UCLA Sports Information; 17, 18, AP/Wide World; 21, Courtesy UCLA Sports Information; 22, 25, AP/Wide World; 26, ©Jonathan Kirn/Sports Photo Masters, Inc.; 29, ©David L. Johnson/ Sportschrome East/West; 30, Reuters/Bettmann; 32, 35, Focus on Sports, Inc.; 36 (top), Reuters/Bettmann; 36 (bottom), J.D. Cuban/Allsport USA; 38, 40, Focus on Sports, Inc.; 43, Sportschrome East/ West; 44 (both photos), Courtesy UCLA Sports Information; 45 (left), AP/Wide World; 45 (right), ©Noren Trotman/Sports Photo Masters, Inc.; 46, Focus on Sports, Inc.; 47 ©Scott Cunningham/Sportschrome East/West

Editorial Staff

Project Editor: Mark Friedman
Design: Herman Adler Design Group
Photo Editor: Jan Izzo

Library of Congress Cataloging-in-Publication Data

Cox, Ted.
    Reggie Miller : basketball sharpshooter / by Ted Cox.
      p. cm. – (Sports stars)
    ISBN 0-516-04393-5
    1. Miller, Reggie, 1965– —Juvenile literature. 2. Basketball
players—United States—Biography—Juvenile literature.
I. Title. II. Series.
GV884.M556C69   1995
796.323'092–dc20   94-1105
[B]   CIP
                                       AC

REGGIE MILLER

BASKETBALL SHARPSHOOTER

Reggie Miller is a hard guy to figure out. He's a California beach boy, but he lives in the Indiana heartland. He's tall and skinny, but he is known for his toughness. He's a dead-eye shooter, but he takes pride in team defense. He likes to "talk trash" with his opponents, but he has the discipline to be one of the best free-throw shooters in basketball.

Reggie likes to attract attention on the court, but away from the game, he lives a quiet life with his wife, Marita, in Indianapolis, Indiana. When he first came to Indiana, he was called brash, and he nicknamed himself "Hollywood." But when he was given his own television show, he did not showcase himself. He turned it into a talk show for kids.

Reggie Miller was born on August 24, 1965, in Riverside, California. He was the fourth of five children in an athletic family. But when Reggie was born, doctors thought he would never play sports. His hips were twisted so that his legs and ankles turned inward. Reggie had to wear steel braces on his legs until he was four years old. Everyone thought he would never be able to run like other children.

"Yes he will," said his mother, Carrie. "I know he will."

Reggie remembers, "I was always in the house with my mom. I was in the kitchen with her, a real momma's boy." His brothers and sisters would be playing outside, and Reggie's mother would reassure him that he would eventually be able to join them. "She'd always say, 'You'll be out there soon, honey. You've just got to get your legs stronger.' She was so optimistic. My parents never told me anything negative. They told me, 'You will walk. You will run. You will play basketball.'"

Reggie's brother, Darrel Miller, played for the California Angels.

As the years passed, Reggie did grow strong enough to play outside. But by then, he had some catching up to do. His older brother, Darrel, was on his way to becoming an excellent baseball player. He eventually reached the major leagues and played several seasons with the California Angels. But it was Reggie's older sister, Cheryl, who inherited their father's love of basketball.

Saul Miller, Sr., was a computer systems analyst for a hospital. He had been a college basketball star in Memphis, Tennessee, before moving to California. Reggie and Cheryl were the two kids closest in age, and they were always playing basketball together. Cheryl often beat her brother in hoops. She got so good that she beat the son of the basketball coach one-on-one in junior high school. When the coach wouldn't let her join the boys' team, Saul Miller organized a girls' team. He said, "In our family, we all have to support each other, help everyone improve."

Meanwhile, Reggie was always practicing, even when there was no one to play with. "When I was growing up, my father had a little area of concrete for our backyard basket," Reggie remembers. "My first goal was to master every shot in that area. After I did that, I said, 'Dad, we need more concrete.' Eventually we had an area that went back maybe 22 feet from the basket. Any more than that was in my mother's rose garden, and I shot from there, too. I apologize, but it paid off."

Carrie Miller wasn't very happy about what was happening to her roses. But she had to smile when she saw Cheryl and Reggie play basketball. Reggie was good, but Cheryl was getting even more attention. Reggie had to learn to play in Cheryl's shadow. He scored 39 points in one high-school game, but on the same day, Cheryl had an incredible 105 points for the girls' team.

Reggie's sister, Cheryl, was one of the best female basketball players of all time.

"Overcoming my sister's shadow has been the biggest obstacle in my life," Reggie says. But playing rough sports with a body that was growing up tall and thin was almost as hard. It seemed Reggie always had to prove himself. So he started acting tough.

"I was always getting knocked down," Reggie remembers. "But I would never show the other kids they hurt me. I'd get up and say, 'Is that your best shot? Come on, hit me harder.'"

When Reggie entered college at the University of California at Los Angeles (UCLA), his sister was already a big star. She led the University of Southern California (USC) women's basketball team to back-to-back national championships. Later, she starred on the U.S. Olympic team that won the women's basketball gold medal in the 1984 Summer Olympics. People were saying that Cheryl was the greatest woman basketball player in the world.

Above: Cheryl Miller
and her parents celebrate
after Cheryl led the U.S.
women's basketball team
to a gold medal in the
1984 Summer Olympics.
Right: Meanwhile, Reggie's
fame was growing at UCLA.

UCLA

Reggie, meanwhile, had trouble adjusting to the college game as a freshman. One writer joked that Reggie was the first player in UCLA history who couldn't outplay his own sister.

Reggie said, "I'll always be her little brother, because no guy is ever going to match what Cheryl did. But she gave me something to reach for." Cheryl is now the women's basketball coach at USC, and her fame has not faded. In 1995, she was elected to the Basketball Hall of Fame. Through it all, Cheryl and Reggie have remained very close. "Not only is she my older sister," says Reggie, "she's my best friend."

Cheryl Miller gives instructions to her team as head coach of the USC women's basketball team.

Reggie holds the MVP trophy after helping UCLA clinch the 1985
National Invitation Tournament.

Reggie was finding his own ways of getting attention playing with the UCLA Bruins. UCLA has a great basketball tradition. From 1964 to 1975, the school won ten college titles in 12 years under legendary coach John Wooden. After Wooden retired, however, the Bruins began losing. They were counting on Reggie to lead them back to the top.

As a sophomore, Reggie's play improved dramatically over his first college season. The Bruins won the 1985 National Invitation Tournament (a post-season tournament for good teams that don't make the NCAA championships), and Reggie was named tournament MVP. It was the Bruins' first championship of any sort since the John Wooden era.

Reggie was developing a reputation as a big-game player. "I love to be in the pressure cooker," he said. "If there's a last shot to be taken, a last rebound to be got...let it be me. I've been there. I'm not afraid. I'm a leader."

As a junior, Reggie averaged 26 points per game, fourth-highest in the nation. In his senior year, college basketball added the three-point shot for the first time. Reggie proved especially deadly at shooting these long-range baskets. He beat Notre Dame with a last-minute three-pointer. Said UCLA coach Walt Hazzard, "If you want to be an All-American, those are the kinds of shots you have to make." Local newspapers called the three-point line "Reggie range."

Playing in a big city like Los Angeles was good for Reggie. He was bold and outspoken, and he loved the media attention he received. He also developed a strong friendship with Los Angeles Lakers All-Stars such as Earvin "Magic" Johnson and Michael Cooper. They'd play pickup games at UCLA. "Magic and Michael Cooper took me under their wings," Reggie said. "They told me to watch, listen, and learn."

By the end of his college career, Reggie had become one of the most dangerous scorers in the game. He could shoot from the outside or drive to the hoop.

Yet Reggie was also developing a reputation for taunting opposing players and fans. Sometimes, Reggie got too much attention, and fans would boo and jeer him. Reggie didn't care about being booed. "It shows they're thinking of me," he said. "But they get awfully quiet when I hit those three-pointers."

As a senior at UCLA, Reggie's scoring average actually dipped a little to 22.3 points per game. But he led UCLA to the Pac-10 Conference title and the NCAA tournament. When Reggie graduated in 1987, he was the second-leading scorer in UCLA history, behind only Lew Alcindor (the legendary center who later changed his name to Kareem Abdul-Jabbar).

Despite his college accomplishments, pro scouts doubted Reggie's NBA potential. "They thought I had a bad [senior] season," Reggie now says. "We were more team-oriented my last year. Hey, I'll gladly score less and win 25 games, than score more and win 16."

In the 1987 NBA draft, Reggie was chosen 11th by the Indiana Pacers. "I was full of confidence when I got drafted," Reggie said years later. "I knew I could play this game. Now a lot of people wish they would've drafted me....I like to show people they were wrong."

Although Reggie was confident, Indiana Pacers fans were unhappy. They wanted the team to draft Steve Alford, a college star at nearby Indiana University. Reggie had to prove himself all over again. In his first season as a pro, he averaged ten points a game and made the second-team NBA All-Rookie Team. Reggie also hit 61 three-pointers to break Larry Bird's rookie record. Even Bird was convinced about Reggie, saying, "I thought the Pacers blew it when they drafted him, but he's a tough player."

Reggie drives against Larry Bird, who complimented Reggie for his toughness as a rookie.

Early in his career, Reggie learned not to tangle with Michael Jordan.

Still, another NBA great remained unconvinced.
The Pacers were in the same division as the
Chicago Bulls. That meant Reggie often played
head-to-head against Michael Jordan. From their
first game, Reggie tried to rise to the occasion.
"I love challenges," Reggie said. "And playing
against Michael is the biggest chess match in
the world."

Reggie's teammate, Chuck Person, played
a trick on him at the start of the 1988-89 season.
Person told Reggie to try to annoy Michael and
take him out of his game. So in an exhibition
game, Reggie started talking trash with Michael.
Everybody who had been in the league a few years
knew that making Michael Jordan mad was the
wrong thing to do. Sure enough, Michael scored
36 points off Reggie. When the players were
walking off the floor, Michael scolded Reggie,
"Don't you ever talk trash with me again."

An embarrassed Reggie remembers, "I was
like, 'You are absolutely right, Mr. Jordan.'"

★ ★ ★

Reggie was learning other lessons, too. He was quickly becoming an outstanding NBA player. In his third season, 1989-90, Reggie became Indiana's leading scorer, with 24.6 points per game. He made the All-Star team. Even more important, the Pacers finished with a winning record of 42-40 and made the playoffs for the first time in three years.

During the next two years, however, the Pacers remained a mediocre team and were eliminated early in the playoffs. The team was treading water. Reggie was one of its few consistent players. He averaged more than 20 points a game every year, and in 1992-93, he led the NBA in three-pointers. But he still made mistakes. In one tough contest, Reggie and Michael Jordan got into a fight on the court. Reggie was thrown out of the game, and Michael was suspended for a game.

"If there was one thing that almost tarnished my reputation for good, it was the fight with Michael Jordan," Reggie now says. "Michael is the best guy, everyone's favorite. But [I had] so much frustration built up with the Bulls." Michael and Reggie have become friends, but back then their feud was a serious matter. In Chicago, fans booed Reggie constantly.

But Reggie didn't much mind how opposing fans treated him. He says, "I love being the villain. And I love being booed. It really gets me going....That's OK. I'll be the bad guy."

Although he can annoy his opponents and opposing fans,
Reggie's teammates agree he's a terrific, generous guy.

But his teammates and coaches know a different Reggie. "He's not a good guy, he's a great guy," says Pacers coach Larry Brown. "Especially with the kids. You see him at the summer camp and it's not just the star showing up to give a few tips. He's there working with the kids all day."

"On the road, he's always taking the ballboys out to dinner," adds Pacers president Donnie Walsh. "He's really this sweet guy, not at all the braggart, but a very easy guy to be around."

Off the court, Reggie was becoming known as a friendly, helpful person. For instance, he liked to visit children in hospitals. "I understand what it's like for a kid to be trapped inside behind four walls," Reggie says, recalling his difficult childhood.

But on the court, Reggie continued building up his bad-boy image. In the 1993 playoffs, Reggie got into a feud with New York Knicks guard John Starks. In one game, Reggie made Starks so mad that Starks bumped Reggie in the chin with his forehead. Starks was ejected from the game. Reggie went on to score 36 points, and the Pacers won the game. But it was the Pacers' only win in the series, and they were again eliminated from the playoffs.

Reggie still needed to learn when it was okay to jokingly talk trash and when to let his playing skills talk for him. "I think trash-talking jacks me up," he says. "It gives me security. I know I'm not the best. I'm lucky to be here. So a lot of times on the court I'll talk to myself — for reassurance."

After being eliminated by the Knicks, it was apparent that the entire Pacers team needed more discipline. So Larry Brown was hired as the team's head coach. Brown drilled the Pacers on team unity and built a strong team defense.

Reggie and rival John Starks (left)

Left: Head coach Larry Brown worked on Indiana's defense, which helped them surge forward in the 1994 playoffs.

Above: Reggie and teammate Vern Fleming celebrate their stunning first-round upset of the Orlando Magic.

Reggie took well to the new emphasis on defense. "I knew I could always play defense," Reggie said, "but because I shot the three so well...people thought that's all I could do."

In the Pacers' first season under Coach Brown, they started off a dismal 16-23. But in the second half of the season, they were one of the hottest teams in the NBA. They finished the regular season at 47-35. Then, they surprised Shaquille O'Neal and the Orlando Magic by sweeping them in the first round of the 1994 playoffs. It was the first time the Pacers had won a playoff series since they joined the NBA. A jubilant Reggie said, "When you've been on the bottom and finally taste success, it's the best feeling in the world."

The Pacers weren't finished surprising people. In the next round, they met the Atlanta Hawks, who had the best record in the Eastern Conference. With Reggie's bull's-eye shooting and the team playing excellent defense, the Pacers eliminated the Hawks in six games. In the third round, Indiana would face the New York Knicks for the right to go to the NBA Finals.

The Knicks won the first two games in New York, but the Pacers got even with two straight wins in Indiana. Then came Game Five in New York's Madison Square Garden. Reggie and John Starks had continued their feud throughout the series. And from the Garden's front row, Starks had a loud ally — movie director Spike Lee, a dedicated and intense Knicks fan.

The Knicks led 70-58 going into the fourth quarter. Reggie was not having a lucky shooting night. He said, "It seemed like every one of my [shots] had gone in and out. I made a decision that I was going to shoot us right back in the game or shoot us right out of it."

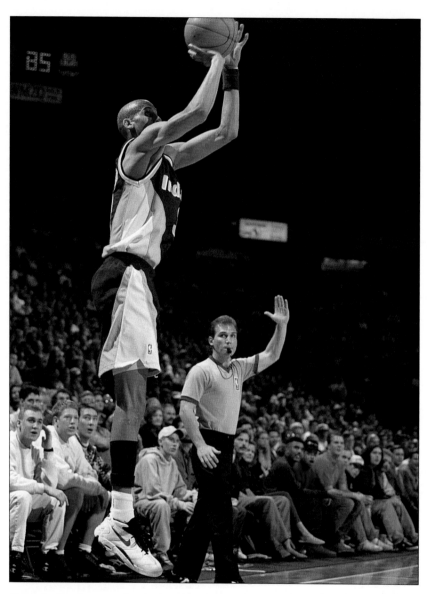

Reggie had a magical shooting touch in Game Five against the Knicks, making him an overnight hero.

Reggie took the floor in the fourth quarter and put on one of the great shooting displays in NBA playoff history. He made a record five three-pointers and scored 25 points in the final period. Reggie's fifth "three" came from 27 feet away, and it clinched the Pacers' dramatic victory. With every shot he made, Reggie carried on his shouting match with number-one Knicks fan, Spike Lee. For standing up to the tough New York crowd and single-handedly winning the game, Reggie became an overnight hero across the country.

Despite Reggie's heroics in Game Five, the Knicks were too tough in the end. New York won the final two games of the series. After the Pacers were eliminated, Reggie was in tears in the locker room. But he had proven himself once and for all to NBA players and fans.

That summer, Reggie joined Dream Team II as one of its three team captains. He was named to the all-tournament team while leading the U.S. squad to the gold medal at the World Basketball Championships in Toronto. On the medal stand, Reggie extended his arms as if to embrace the Canadian fans.

The player who used to be booed is now a fan favorite. "It's hard to get used to the cheering," Reggie says. "I've been the underdog so long. I was really never that highly touted and always seemed to be playing in the shadow of a superstar. So I kept battling uphill."

Reggie has learned when to act tough and when to play skillfully, when to talk trash and when to let his game talk for him. That has made it harder for opponents to figure him out. But as basketball fans get to know him better, they are growing to like him more and more.

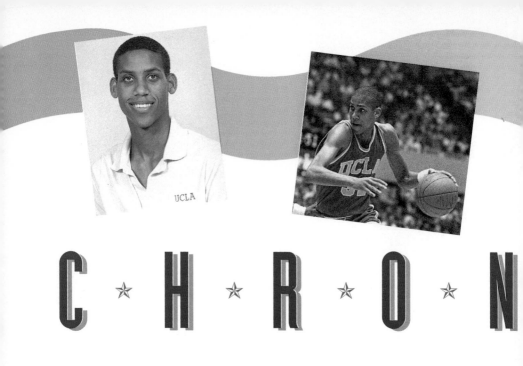

C ✦ H ✦ R ✦ O ✦ N

1965 • Reginald Wayne (Reggie) Miller is born to Saul and Carrie Miller in Riverside, California.

1979-83 • Attends Riverside Polytechnic High School.

1983 • Enters University of California, Los Angeles (UCLA).

1984-85 • As a sophomore, leads UCLA to NIT championship; named tournament MVP.

1985-86 • Averages 25.9 points per game, fourth in the nation.

1986-87 • Finishes college career with 2,095 points.
• Leads UCLA to Pac-10 conference title.
• Chosen 11th in NBA draft by Indiana Pacers.

1987-88 • Sets rookie season record with 61 three-point baskets; named to NBA All-Rookie Second Team.

1989-90 • Named to NBA All-Star team.

O ✶ L ✶ O ✶ G ✶ Y

1992-93 • Leads NBA with 167 three-point baskets; scores 57 points in one game.

1993-94 • Tops 10,000 career points and becomes Pacers all-time leading scorer.
• Leads Pacers to NBA Eastern Conference Finals; sets NBA playoff record with five three-point baskets in one quarter of a game against New York Knicks; becomes Pacers all-time leading playoff scorer.
• Named co-captain of Dream Team II and helps U.S. team win gold medal at World Basketball Championships.

1994-95 • Elected as a starter to the Eastern Conference All-Star team.
• Leads Pacers to Eastern Conference Finals, where they are eliminated by the Orlando Magic.

REGGIE MILLER

Reginald Wayne Miller

Nickname **Reggie**
Date of Birth **August 24, 1965**
Place of Birth **Riverside, California**
Home **Indianapolis, Indiana**
Height **6-foot-7**
Weight **185 pounds**
College **University of California, Los Angeles (UCLA)**
Pro Team **Indiana Pacers**
Famous siblings
Sister **Cheryl Miller** (basketball Hall of Famer) Brother **Darrell Miller** (baseball player)
NBA All-Star **1990, 1995**

 NBA STATISTICS

Season	Team	Scoring Average	3-Point Baskets	Assists	Steals
1987-88	Indiana	10.0	61	132	53
1988-89	Indiana	16.0	98	227	93
1989-90	Indiana	24.6	150	311	110
1990-91	Indiana	22.6	112	331	109
1991-92	Indiana	20.7	129	314	105
1992-93	Indiana	21.2	167	262	120
1993-94	Indiana	19.9	123	248	119
1994-95	Indiana	19.6	195	242	98
Total (8 seasons)		**19.4**	**1,035**	**2,067**	**807**

★ ★ ★

About the Author

Ted Cox is a Chicago journalist who works at the *Daily Southtown*. He has covered sports for the *Chicago Reader* and *Chicago* magazine. He worked at United Press International and holds a B.S. in journalism from the University of Illinois at Urbana-Champaign. He lives in Chicago with his wife, Catherine, and their daughter, Sadie.